DUSK RINGS A BELL

a European Premiere by Stephen Belber

First performance as part of HighTide Festival 2011,
The Old Printworks, Halesworth, Suffolk on 28 April 2011

World premiere presented by Atlantic Theater Company,
New York City, 2010

Presented by special arrangement with
International Creative Management

First performance at the Edinburgh Festival Fringe on 5 August 2011

Leading Corporate Sponsor

LANSONS
communications

LOTTERY FUNDED

Old Possums
Practical Trust
www.old-possums-practical-trust.org.uk

Genesis
FOUNDATION

Dusk Rings A Bell

A European Premiere by Stephen Belber

A HighTide I Escalator East to Edinburgh 2011 Production
in association with Watford Palace Theatre

RAY	Paul Blair
MOLLY	Katherine Kingsley
Director	Steven Atkinson
Design	takis
Lighting	Matt Prentice
Sound	Steven Mayo
Music	Tom Mills
Voice	John Tucker
Assistant Director	Rob Drummer
Casting Director	Charlotte Bevan
Production Manager	Jae Forrester
Stage Manager	Kate Margretts
Press Representation	Mark Borkowski	020 7193 8705

HighTide wishes to thank Claudia West, Kate Madden,
Brigid Larmour, Jason King at the 02 Centre NW3 and
Clare Parsons and Tony Langham at Lansons Communications
for their ongoing support of HighTide.

Cast

Paul Blair (*Ray*)

For HighTide: *Lidless* (HighTide Festival 2010).

Recent theatre credits include: *Caledonia* (National Theatre of Scotland); *Carthage Must Be Destroyed* (Theatre Royal Bath); *Realism* (National Theatre of Scotland); *The Tempest* (Tron Theatre, Glasgow); *A Lie of the Mind, Macbeth, Scenes from an Execution* (Dundee Rep); *Anna Karenina* (Lyceum Theatre, Edinburgh); *East Coast Chicken Supper* (Traverse Theatre, Edinburgh); *Flight* (National Theatre, London).

Television credits include: *The Day of the Triffids, Taggart, Dear Green Place, Sea of Souls, This Morning with Richard, Not Judy, Ruth Rendell Mysteries, Bumping the Odds, Ruffian Hearts, Takin' Over the Asylum.*

Film credits include: *Clive Barker's Book of Blood, Outpost, Hallam Foe, This Year's Love.*

Katherine Kingsley (*Molly*)

Recent theatre credits include: *The 25th Annual Putnam County Spelling Bee* (Donmar Warehouse); *Aspects of Love* (Menier Chocolate Factory); Olivier nominated for *Piaf* (Donmar Warehouse); *The 39 Steps* (Liverpool Playhouse/tour); *The Black and White Ball* (King's Head); *Hobson's Choice* (Chichester Festival Theatre); *Habeus Corpus* (Northcott Theatre); *The Canterbury Tales, The Memory of Water* (Bristol Old Vic); *Suddenly at Home* (Theatre Royal, Windsor); *High Society, Saucy Jack and the Space Vixens* (West End).

Television credits include: *The Bill, Hollyoaks, Jane Hall's Big Bad Bus Ride, Telephone Detective, Operation Good Guys.*

Film credits include: *Weekend, Days of the Siren, Now We Are Three, 100 Second Marriage.*

Company

Stephen Belber (Writer)

As a playwright, Stephen Belber's work has been produced on Broadway and in over twenty-five countries.

His plays include: *Match* (Tony nomination for Frank Langella); *Dusk Rings A Bell* (Atlantic Theater Company); *Tape* (Naked Angels NY/LA/London); *McReele* (Roundabout Theater); *A Small, Melodramatic Story* (Labyrinth Theater Company); *Geometry of Fire* (Rattlestick); *Fault Lines* (Cherry Lane); *One Million Butterflies* (Primary Stages); *Carol Mulroney* (Huntington Theater Company). He was an Associate Writer on *The Laramie Project* (Drama Desk and Lortel nominations) and co-writer on the more recent *Laramie Project: Ten Years Later*. He is a member of both Tectonic Theater Project and the Labyrinth Theater Company.

Work for film includes: *Tape* (directed by Richard Linklater); *The Laramie Project* (Associate Writer/Emmy Nomination for screenwriting); *Drifting Elegant* and *Management*, which he also directed, starring Jennifer Aniston and Steve Zahn. He is currently developing screen adaptations of both *Match* and *McReele*.

Work for television includes: *Rescue Me* and *Law and Order SVU* (staff writer).

Steven Atkinson (Director)

Training: Read Film and Theatre at Reading University and then interned at Hampstead Theatre following graduation in 2005. He became Literary Manager of Hull Truck Theatre in 2006 and then Artistic Director of HighTide Festival Theatre in 2007.

Direction for HighTide: *Incoming* by Andrew Motion (HighTide Festival 2011/Latitude Festival/Aldeburgh Poetry Festival); *Dusk Rings A Bell* by Stephen Belber (HighTide Festival 2011/Edinburgh Festival/Watford Palace Theatre); *Lidless* by Frances Ya-Chu Cowhig (HighTide Festival 2010/Edinburgh Festival/West End); *Muhmah* by Jesse Weaver (HighTide Festival 2009) and *The Pitch* by Nick Payne (Latitude Festival).

Other direction includes: *The Afghan and the Penguin* by Michael Hastings (BBC Radio 4); *Freedom Trilogy* by various (Hull Truck Theatre), *Sexual Perversity in Chicago* by David Mamet (Edinburgh Festival).

Awards include: a Fringe First for *Lidless*, two SOLT Stage One bursaries for *Lidless* and *Stovepipe*, a Whatsonstage Award nomination for Best Off-West End Production for *Stovepipe* and Esquire's Brilliant Brits 2009.

Rob Drummer (Assistant Director)

Training: MA Advanced Theatre Practice, Directing, Central School of Speech and Drama.

For HighTide: Assistant Director, *Incoming* (HighTide Festival 2011).

Directing credits include: *People You May Know* (York Theatre Royal); *Whose Cloud is it Anyway?* (Debunked, People Show Studios); *A Girl in a Car With a Man* (Contact Theatre, Manchester); *A Question of Everything* (Sackville Building, Manchester); *Top Girls* (John Thaw Theatre, Manchester); *The Yellow Wallpaper* (Manchester Museum); *Dans la Mémoire de Mon Corps* (Mantis Ensemble).

Assistant directing credits include: *The Train Driver* (Hampstead Theatre, London).

Rob is Resident Assistant Director at HighTide, working in and across the Literary, Production and Warehouse departments and is also Curator of Horseplay Arts Club.

Steven Mayo (Sound Designer)

For HighTide: *Lidless* (E4 Underbelly, Edinburgh, 2010/Trafalgar Studios, 2011), *Muhmah, Guardians, Fixer* (HighTide Festival 2009); *I Caught Crabs in Walberswick* (HighTide Festival 2008/Bush Theatre, London/Pleasance Cavern, Edinburgh); *Stovepipe* (HighTide Festival 2008/National Theatre, London/Bush Theatre); *Weightless, You Were After Poetry, Lyre and Ned & Sharon* (HighTide Festival 2007).

Other theatre credits include: *Flesh and Blood & Fish and Fowl* (as Associate Sound Designer) *Flyboy is alone again this Christmas, Cabaret Simon* (Pit Theatre, Barbican); *Our Share of Tomorrow* (Edinburgh 10/York Theatre Royal); *The Line, Miniaturists, Silence* (Arcola Theatre, London); *Public Property, Ordinary Dreams, Sh*t M*x, Snowbound* (Trafalgar Studios, London); *Well* (Apollo Theatre, London); *Fight Face* (Lyric Hammersmith Studio/Decibel Festival, Manchester); *Lie of the Land, Lough/Rain* (Edinburgh/Arcola Theatre/York Playhouse); *Hangover Square, Eden's Empire* (Finborough Theatre, London); *Absolutely Frank* (Queen's Theatre, Hornchurch); *Jack and the Beanstalk*; (Barbican, London); *Romeo and Juliet* (Battersea Arts Centre); *Future/Perfect* (Soho Theatre, London); *Mythomania* (White Bear Theatre, London); *Tale of Two Cities, Cinderella* (Guildhall School of Music and Drama); *Dr Foster* (Menier Chocolate Factory, London).

Composition includes: *Breathing Corpses, Soft Armour* (Theatre Souk); *Love & Money* (Arts Ed); *Guardians, Fixer* (HighTide Festival 2009); *Simpatico* (Old Red Lion, London); *Absolutely Frank* (Queen's Theatre, Hornchurch).

www.stevemayo.co.uk

Tom Mills (Music)

For HighTide: *Lidless, Ditch, Moscow Live* (HighTide Festival 2010).

Other theatre credits include: *Electra, Breathing Irregular, The Kreutzer Sonata, Unbroken* (Gate Theatre, London); *A Midsummer Night's Dream, Edward Gant's Amazing Feats of Loneliness* (Headlong); *Dick Whittington and his Cat* (Lyric Hammersmith); *Prince of Denmark, The Eternal Not* (National Theatre, London); *Wanderlust* (Royal Court Theatre, London) *Oliver Twist, The Grimm Brothers' Circus, The Jungle Book, Metropolis* (The Egg, Bath); *Elektra* (Young Vic, London); *Macbeth* (Regent's Park Open Air Theatre).

Radio credits include: *The Afghan and the Penguin* (BBC Radio 4)

Matt Prentice (Lighting Designer)

Trained at Bristol Old Vic.

For HighTide: *I Caught Crabs in Walberswick* (HighTide Festival 2008/Edinburgh Festival/Bush Theatre, London); *Switzerland, Certain Dark Things, Stovepipe* (HighTide Festival 2008), *Fixer, Guardians, Muhmah* (HighTide Festival 2009), *Ditch, Moscow Live* (HighTide Festival 2010), *Lidless* (HighTide Festival 2010/E4 Underbelly, Edinburgh, 2010/Trafalgar Studios, 2011).

Other theatre credits include: *Parade* (South Side, Edinburgh); *A Chorus Line* (Shaw Theatre, London); *The House of Bernarda Alba* (The Players' Theatre, London); *The Young People's Theatre Company Showcase* (Gielgud Theatre, London); *Faust* (Punchdrunk and the National Theatre) *Peter Pan* (The Assembly Room, Derby); *Masque of the Red Death* (Punchdrunk at Battersea Arts Centre).

Awards include: Best Production Design, Critics' Circle Awards 2006 for *Faust*.

Matt is Head of Lighting at the Royal Academy of Dramatic Art and was previously the Head of Lighting Design at the Mountview Academy of Theatre Arts.

takis (Design)

For HighTide: *Lidless* (HighTide Festival 2010/E4 Underbelly, Edinburgh, 2010/Trafalgar Studios, 2011); *Ditch, Moscow Live* (HighTide Festival 2010); *Guardians, Fixer, Muhmah* (HighTide Festival 2009); *Stovepipe* (National Theatre, London, 2009/HighTide Festival 2008); *I Caught Crabs in Walberswick* (HighTide Festival 2008/Edinburgh Festival/Bush Theatre, London); *Switzerland, Certain Dark Things* (HighTide Festival 2008).

Other theatre credits include: *The Early Bird* (Finborough Theatre, London); *Signs of a Star Shaped Diva* (Theatre Royal Stratford East/National Tour); *The Marriage Bed* (Hong Kong Academy for Performing Arts/NY Sanford Meisner Theatre); *Invasion* (Soho Theatre, London); *Scenes from the Big Picture, Sing Yer Heart Out for the Lads, Installation 496* (RADA); *Marat/Sade* (Jermyn Street Theatre, London); *Crazy Lady* (Drill Hall/Contact Theatre, Manchester); *Nikolina* (Pleasance Courtyard, Edinburgh Festival Fringe); *Schweyk in the Second World War* (Theatre Duisburg); *Medea* (Ancient Greek Theatre of Syracusa).

Installations/site specific productions include: *Forgotten Peacock* (Design Museum/The Brunswick, London); *The Tempest* (Hobbs Factory, London); *Goldfish* (Paris Fashion Week); *Mythological Installation Oedipus* (Museum of Contemporary Art, Bucharest); *Visual Performance in Baroque Spirit* (Venice Carnival).

Music performances include: *A Tale of Two Cities* (Theatre Royal, Brighton), *Maria Callas – Vissi D'arte; Vissi D'amore* (Barbican, London); *Choruses: Eternal Service to Beauty* (Ancient Theatre of Epidaurus/ Frankfurt Opera House); *In the Light of the Night* (Ancient Theatre of Epidaurus); *Nikos Skalkotas: a Celebration* (Queen Elizabeth Hall).

www.takis.info

 HighTide

HighTide's *Stovepipe*: One of *The Sunday Times'* Ten Best Theatre Productions of the Decade

A Brief History

Founded in 2007, HighTide Festival Theatre is a not-for-profit theatre company that produces leading-standard contemporary new writing theatre for audiences in the East of England, nationally, and internationally. Our productions premiere in the annual HighTide Festival Season in Suffolk, and we collaborate with regional partners including Aldeburgh Music, DanceEast, The Poetry Trust and the Latitude Festival to produce work. HighTide's work has transferred nationally and internationally, including to London with the Bush Theatre (2008), National Theatre (2009), Old Vic Theatre (2010), the West End (2011), to the Edinburgh Festival (2010/11) and internationally to the Australian National Play Festival (2010). We develop emerging playwrights and directors year-round through our Warehouse, which includes the Genesis Laboratory in London and the Escalator Laboratory spanning the eastern region.

The first HighTide Festival in 2007 premiered eight short plays written by Tom Basden, Steven Bloomer, Sarah Cuddon, Sam Holcroft, Matthew Morrison, Pericles Snowdon, Megan Walsh and Iain Weatherby.

Tom Basden's *Assembly* then transferred to Hay-on-Wye Festival 2008.

The second HighTide Festival in 2008 premiered four plays written by Adam Brace, Joel Horwood, Nick Payne and the fourth devised by You Need Me.

Joel Horwood's *I Caught Crabs in Walberswick* transferred to the 2008 Edinburgh Festival, a UK tour, and the Bush Theatre, in a co-production with Eastern Angles.

Adam Brace's *Stovepipe* transferred to the West 12 Centre in London as a found-space production in collaboration with the National Theatre and Bush Theatre in March 2009. *The Sunday Times* listed this as one of The Ten Best Theatre Productions of the Decade.

Nick Payne's *The Pitch* premiered at Latitude Festival 2008, Suffolk.

The third HighTide Festival in 2009 premiered three plays written by Lydia Adetunji, Lucy Caldwell and Jesse Weaver.

Lydia Adetunji's *Fixer* and Adam Brace's *Stovepipe* transferred to the National Play Festival in Brisbane, Australia, in January 2010. *Fixer* was shortlisted for the Meyer Whitworth Award.

The fourth HighTide Festival in 2010 premiered three plays written by Serge Cartwright, Frances Ya-Chu Cowhig and Beth Steel. Serge Cartwright's *Moscow Live* was shortlisted for the 2010 John Whiting Award.

Beth Steel's *Ditch* transferred to The Old Vic Tunnels in London, in a co-production with The Old Vic, in May 2010. *Ditch* was shortlisted for the 2010 John Whiting Award.

Dominic Mitchell's *The Theatre EP*, conceived by Natalie Ibu, premiered at Latitude Festival 2010, Suffolk.

Frances Ya-Chu Cowhig's *Lidless* transferred to the 2010 Edinburgh Festival, where it won a Fringe First Award before transferring to the Trafalgar Studios, London in March 2011.

The Fifth HighTide Festival, in April and May 2011 premiered *Midnight Your Time* by Adam Brace, *Incoming* by Andrew Motion, *Dusk Rings A Bell* by Stephen Belber, and a new musical comedy, *Nicked*, book and lyrics by Richard Marsh and music by Rogue Nouveau (aka Natalia Sheppard).

Andrew Motion's *Incoming* transferred to Latitude Festival 2011 before transferring to the Aldeburgh Poetry Festival in November 2011.

Stephen Belber's *Dusk Rings A Bell* transferred to the 2011 Edinburgh Festival before transferring to the Watford Palace Theatre in September 2011.

Adam Brace's *Midnight Your Time* transferred to the 2011 Edinburgh Festival.

For more information please visit: **www.hightide.org.uk**

HighTide is a registered charity and is dependant on the ongoing support of individuals, businesses and charitable trusts & foundations.

Friends of the Festival have exclusive access to HighTide. To get involved, please contact hello@hightide.org.uk

HighTide: A major initiative of
Old Possums
Practical Trust
www.old-possums-practical-trust.org.uk

LOTTERY FUNDED

Genesis
FOUNDATION

Subsidised rehearsal space for HighTide Festival Theatre provided by
JERWOOD **SPACE**

Foreword

I first met Stephen Belber in New York City in 2011, two days after Mayor Michael Bloomberg announced that the city had experienced the snowiest January in history, with a thick blanket of snow covering everywhere. We met in a coffee shop on 7th in the West Village and, like all good blind dates, I emailed him a description of my appearance. There was no need; I was the only New Yorker wearing Converse and a blazer-sans-overcoat.

When Stephen and I met he had already granted HighTide Festival Theatre the rights to produce the European premiere of his play *Dusk Rings A Bell*, following its premiere off-Broadway at the Atlantic Theater the previous summer. Kara Manning, an American playwright who had flown to London to develop her play through HighTide's Genesis Laboratory research and development programme, gave me the play to read. It had reviewed okay in New York. But what had perhaps seemed slight to Americans was to me, a European, a rich and mature play about Americans, and one that in a subtle, dignified way, addressed the root of crimes of hate and, the great American taboo – sexuality.

Over coffee, Stephen revealed two interesting genesis points for this play. Molly was first conceived for Uma Thurman, who in 2000 was filming in a screen adaptation of Stephen's play, *Tape*. Ray came later. Stephen, as a member of the Tectonic Theater Project, had in 1998 been an interviewer on the seminal verbatim play *The Laramie Project*, which is about how the residents of Laramie, Wyoming, grappled with the notorious murder of the gay college student Matthew Shepard. Ten years later, Stephen and other members of Tectonic returned to Laramie to write an epilogue to their play. Ray is Stephen's response to Russell Henderson, one of two young men who severely beat Matthew Shepard and left him to die, tied to a fence on the outskirts of Laramie.

Stephen told a story that when *Dusk Rings A Bell* opened in New York, one or two members of Tectonic who attended the production were concerned that sections of the play blurred the line as to the actual murderer's intentions that night. But this seems to be one of the play's greatest strengths. It acknowledges the complexity of humanity, and dramatises the difficulties of trying to rationalise your own behaviours, and those of others.

Over a second coffee in Union Square in a still snowy New York, Stephen and I continued to discuss his play; me taking notes, and he passing on information. We talked back and forth, opening up the possibilities of this story. Towards the end, Stephen asked me for some paper and my pen and started to write. He scribbled away frantically in silence. Then he stopped, looked up at me, and said, 'I can't fucking believe you're asking me to do a rewrite.' This play was largely formed for the Atlantic Theater with the help of director Sam Gold and his company, but I'm delighted to be able to continue the story abroad.

Steven Atkinson
Artistic Director, HighTide Festival Theatre
London, April 2011

Dusk Rings A Bell took part in the Genesis Laboratory, HighTide's research and development studio, situated in the 02 Centre, NW3, Finchley Road, London

DUSK RINGS A BELL

Stephen Belber

Dusk Rings A Bell was developed at the Ojai Playwrights' Conference, California, in July 2009, with the following cast:

MOLLY	Bess Wohl
RAY	Stephen Belber

It was first performed by Atlantic Theater Company, New York City, on 27 May 2010, with the following cast and creative team:

MOLLY	Kate Walsh
RAY	Paul Sparks
Director	Sam Gold
Set Designer	Takeshi Kata
Lighting Designer	Ben Stanton
Sound Designer	Jill Du Boff
Costume Designer	Theresa Squire
Stage Manager	Erin Maureen Koster
Artistic Director	Neal Pepe
Associate Artistic Director	Christian Parker
Managing Director	Jeffory Lawson
General Manager	Jamie Tyrol

4

Characters

MOLLY
RAY

The props and settings alluded to in this script most likely aren't necessary.

This text went to press before the end of rehearsals and so may differ slightly from the play as performed.

A woman (MOLLY) *stands alone on a stage.*

MOLLY. I'm not one of those people who has difficulty communicating.

It's not something I have trouble with. Which is a fact I take pride in: my ability to articulate; my capacity for intrapersonal comprehension through verbal imagery. I'm by no means an expert. I am not beyond exquisite communication of an otherwise shoddy idea. In fact I occasionally parlay eloquently an absolutely horrid notion. Other times, the need for linguistic clarity will *overwhelm* the message, to the point where I am incessantly elucidating the finer points of my point when there is in fact no point at all.

None of which belies the fact that I'm good at what I do. I'm a communicator, and I use this modicum of talent that God or someone of His ilk bequeathed me in order to make a more-than-decent living. I work for a man named Jeff, who I think would concur when I say he takes pride in his *lack* of any and all communication acuity, even though he, too, is in PR. Actually, that's not fair, he communicates quite well, but he communicates the epic. He is a communicator of great *notions*, and I his semi-elocutious sidekick, brought in three years ago to fill in the blanks with words. I secure the final bolts on the bridge that spans the great divide between notion and namesake. (*Pause.*) And on weekends I occasionally paint.

There's nothing romantic between Jeff and me. Yes, he's handsome, but rarely before six, an hour *after* which I rarely see him. I'd possibly marry Jeff if I saw him more often in the post-six world. *Prior* to six he wears well-made loafers and I like him very much; after six he wears Chuck Taylor high tops and I have a tendency to occasionally fall quite profoundly for him. He keeps them in a closet in his office and if Ron or John or Don or Juan – we're very multi-culti-*shockingly*-gay-friendly – if one of his gregarious, affable, east-coast-semi-educated lackeys comes in pleading for happy-hour accompaniment, Jeff jettisons the loafers and dives into his closet with teenage abandon, heading to the bar in his purple Chucky T's and Brooks Brothers blazer. He drinks schooners of Bud Light and becomes a warm-hearted mensch with a violent streak, which is, of course, right up my proverbial alley. I rarely accompany them. If I do, I stay for two drinks tops and then I beat it. I like my home. The second floor of a Brownstone on Riggs Place, in DC. But I don't have a cat.

The one time I *did* let Jeff 'usher me home', as was the wording of his loquacious offer, we made love. He took everything off but his high tops and I, everything but my friendship ring – which is an ever-present metaphor for my constantly fluctuating relationship with the world and has nothing to do with Jeff in particular. (*Pause.*) It was nice. He's actually a bit of a freak, which is perhaps why I'd marry him, seeing as I'm so thoroughly alienated from my *own* sense of freakishness, which I think Jeff appreciates, or at least momentarily enjoyed that night in a somewhat perverted way. When a freak comes across someone alienated from their freakishness, it freaks them out a bit, in a good way, meaning when Jeff realised I wouldn't take off my metaphorical ring, i.e. the untouchable and utterly calculated distancing mechanism with which I daily greet the world, it actually excited him *more*, which unfortunately led to premature activities on his part that he strove to make up for with a proclivity towards self-regeneration that I can only tip my hat to. (*Pause.*) But enough about Jeff.

Needless to say, I used to have a stuttering problem. Nothing serious, although serious enough for my mother to enlist the services of the very unknown pathologist Dr Richard Laborowitz, a South *Afrikaner* who invariably had a gigantic bowl of dark chocolate sitting on the tiny playtable between us. I lasted two sessions. Stuttering – besides in some cases being a neurophysiologic genetic disorder, is, in others, almost symbolically, a simple yearning for mature articulation. Granted this is partly my own theory, but developmental stuttering is often in part due to a child's desire for communication outstripping their current skill set. A great and guttural *need* to self-express, impeded by a lack of linguistic *chutzpah* – because that's really what it is: the motor skills can't keep up with the complex and highly emotional *explosion* that's occurring inside. This was me: unable to articulate the notion of the emotion.

And everybody stutters in *some* respect: we grow up quicker than we grow up; we understand before we're capable of expression. Which also, for example, explains sex. By age seventeen, we understand the fact that we need human contact – i.e. love – but we're incapable of truly *communicating* that need, so we end up simply screwing everything in sight. Both are examples of us hammering away unsuccessfully at the Gibraltar of human connection, famished for love but reduced to the feeble endeavours of ceaseless stuttering and simple-minded screwing. I myself went from being a stutterer to a screwer almost overnight. Actually, that's not true, there was a year there around age fifteen when I was a *non*-stuttering non-screwer who consistently and joyfully masturbated to *The Smiths*, but… 'tis another story.

When I was fourteen, I figured out the key to life. I stopped stuttering – overnight.

The year was 1985, the month – August, the place – Bethany Beach, Delaware.

My parents Bob and Bobbie – I swear to God, all their friends thought that was 'just so nifty'. They were like *nerdy* hippies. My mom's wedding attire included a purple sash; my dad wore a tux with DayGlo purple socks. Bob and Bobbie, having outgrown their group-sex days – which for them entailed fellatio with the TV on – rented a house in Bethany in the summer of '85.

At the time, I was reading a fruitful combination of Virginia Woolf, Kurt Vonnegut and, yes, Mickey Spillane, and basically just wanted to be left alone. Being an only child, I knew how to take care of myself, which isn't to say I was happy, in fact the stuttering was worse than ever and I was into this thing where I was crying myself to sleep, so...

And then I awoke one morning – actually my last morning there that week, and I decided that the stuttering had to stop. It simply had to. So I wrote myself a note. (*Pause.*) I somehow must've realised that if I stuck with things – like my aspiration to live an at least vaguely happy life – I would *need* to, eventually, express myself in the mature modes for which I yearned. It came to me that communication – which for me was the core of the problem – that communication, like my mother's old clothes, my sexuality, my desire to read *Ulysses* – was something I would grow into. Happiness, I guess is what it came down to – *happiness*... was something I would grow into. (*Pause.*) So I wrote myself a note saying something to that effect. And it turned out to be the key.

And I remember... I remember that I read it over to myself out loud several times... and then I decided to hide it some-where. Like a treasure. (*Pause.*) This is kind of stupid. But I hid it like a treasure, and I told myself that when I was thirty-nine – which is the age my mother would always pretend to be once she'd turned forty – that at age thirty-nine, if I was in need of a treasure, I would go back and find it. This note that I wrote to myself. In Bethany Beach, Delaware, when I was fourteen.

Beat. Lights shift.

And so here I am. In a car, twenty-five years later. Going to find my note.

A man (RAY) *enters. He walks to a stool and sits on it. He does not see* MOLLY, *nor she him. Beat. After a moment, she continues.*

As I cross the Chesapeake Bay Bridge, it all starts to come back. Three point two miles, the sprawl as intense today as it was back in those summers when I drove there with my parents. I'm in my Renault, which is tiny but I love it. Jeff and his lackeys give me flack. They say I'm cheap, I say it's French.

It's a Saturday in February, which is nice, although I'm not sure why. I guess I just love Saturdays. I wake up, I have nothing to do. I listen to an African radio show and pretend... that I'm African. It's all very authentic.

By the way the reason I stopped stuttering is because of that note. Hiding it in the rafter above my bunk in that rented house at Bethany, I essentially stopped the next day. I had discovered how to express myself. Period. People do it all the time.

RAY (*almost cutting her off*). I'm pretty sure I know when I'm gonna die. I'll be ninety-two. Fairly content. And then I'll be stabbed by a home-made knife. While in bed. By some young kids who keep yelling, 'Die, you withered old faggot!' And I'll be like, 'But I'm not gay.' But it'll be too late, and they won't seem to care anyway. (*Pause.*) I saw it in a dream, but not a dream I had a lot; in fact I only had it once, but I specifically remember that image: me on the ground, bleeding, being yelled at like that. (*Beat.*) I have a good memory when it comes to certain images, even if I forget where they come from – and even if I'm not even sure they ever really happened.

Like the image of the first time I kissed a girl on the lips in a *deeply* romantic kinda way. Thinking to myself... 'This is... (*Quiet.*) seriously innovative.' I'm sure I'd kissed other girls before then, but not like that. And I don't even remember details except for that her lips were like... syrup. That's the image – I guess it's like a sensual one: kissing a girl with syrup lips, when I was still young, at the end of a long day. (*Pause.*) So once in a blue moon I'll think of that; when tasting syrup.

I can also remember, I *think*, this day when I was two years old and my mom and I watched a rat being torn apart and eaten by a hawk. On a tree branch, on the side of a road near a Pizza Hut. And we just stood beneath it and watched as the rat guts were being, like, completely stripped away, gut by gut, as the hawk devoured its... its meal. I was gonna say its *prey*, but...

MOLLY, *having not heard any of this, immediately continues.*

MOLLY. I haven't been back to this area since my junior year in high school. Beach Week, 1986. Just up the coast from Bethany, Rehoboth is where all the DC and Maryland kids go for their debaucherous little lustcapades. I skipped it my senior year. I'd moved on to the college boys, which is neither braggadocio nor self-hate, but rather just... *realpolitik*. For the next three years I was on a laser-guided mission to fully and uninhibitedly express the meta-sexualised, shit-bent-for-authenticity, soul-hammering and no-longer-stammering zealot within. I screwed with the abandon of a fighter pilot on crank; I soaked up life like it was the last lonely dewdrop on earth; I slurp-sucked new sensation with a degree of ferocity that wild and horny tigresses could only fucking salivate on.

I also put on twenty pounds.

Life since then has... occurred. Post-college angst, professional success, the Gulf War, marriage, divorce, the embrace of my inner child. I suppose I should mention the *Iraq* War, which I guess is the inner child of the Gulf War. (*Pause.*) I'll also add that my parents have died. My dad went first. During the years of my marriage. And then Bobbie, last year. Who died in the most typical of all ways.

The marriage was to a man named Chuck, with whom I was for a period spanning my early thirties to my mid-to-early/ late-*mid* thirties; Chuck, who loved me with an alternating mix of surreal hyperactivity and extremely awkward flakiness, and with whom I shared a divorce after serial arguments over

cereal and should we have kids and *was* Nirvana a better
source of cultural inspiration than Tchaikovsky – and let it be
known that Kurt's the fucking *man*, Chuck... It was after the
divorce that I returned to Washington to work for and sleep
once with Jeff. (*Pause*.) I work at CNN. I'm a vice-president
for media relations for the DC bureau. I've had drinks with
George Stephanopolous; twice; bourbon; *he* paid.

RAY *perhaps shifts slightly in his chair, but* MOLLY *doesn't
particularly notice.*

Twenty-five years later, images of the house are still
ingrained in my mind. Beachfront property, the house itself
emphatically competent, replete with a stuffed and mounted
moosehead, an L-shaped sofa and a bathroom with a shag-
carpet-covered seat to keep your buttocks warm on those
chilly beachfront nights. All in all, a seventies' classic.

Spotting something in the distance.

That could be it.

More modest than I remember. I park on the street and sneak
up and around – dune level – to peek into the main room...
And there it is – the moosehead, jutting forth from a wall
above the fireplace. Everything is just the same.

Silence everywhere. Even the moose. Silent shag, silent sofa,
silent poker table. The dunes a touch less so, a soft wind
gently whistling through them. They're shimmering... and
the sand looks a little sad; which is dumb, but...

Everything's locked, as expected, so I find the bathroom
window, its glass work sandy, blurred, no doubt a little sad. I
stand back, cover my eyes with my right hand and with my
left use my hammer – which I've actually brought along for
this – and SMASH –

Sound of glass breaking.

– reach in, unlock, open and hoist myself, feet first, my
never-realised-slash-never-*to*-be-realised-question mark –
childbearing hips shimmying along behind.

And I land on the shag-endowed toilet for my first official fully-committed crime… if you don't count a fair amount of pot in the eighties, plus having gay friends who 'did sodomy' in Virginia before it became legal in 2003.

RAY. By the way, that thing about the hawk is, like, indelible. My mom and I still refer to it. And I was two. Which is, of course, maybe one of those things where, you know, the only reason you remember it is because you've talked about it so much, but… My mom likes to say it was 'formative', and I'm like, 'Mom.' And she's like, 'What?' And I'm like, 'It was not formative.' And she's like, 'Why not?' And I'm like, 'Because maybe I haven't been fully formed yet.' And she's like, 'Well, that's an issue for your priest.' (*Pause*.) Which it is, but…

MOLLY. Most summer houses in winter are freezing. There's rarely insulation but mostly they're just *emotionally* cold. Like ballrooms at ten a.m.; or airplanes stripped of all their seats; or a family whose only child reads far too many books. (*Pause*.) Point is, they're like the sand: kinda pretty, but undeniably a little sad.

I head down to the bedroom level… enter the room… (*Pause*.) And the bunk bed is no longer there.

There's just a bed. A *bed* bed, new, clean, no doubt '*posturepedic*'. Like the owner splurged in lieu of changing the twenty-year-old shitter shag.

I climb on the bed, tiptoes giving me height to actually touch the ceiling – nudge the panelling… dislodge… reach hand into darkness above where my eyes can see… and grope. I am groping like I've never groped, I am groping like a savage, an infant, like a purple-sash-wearing virgin on the first night of the rest of her life…

MOLLY *gropes… and suddenly she has a many-times-folded piece of paper in her hand.*

YES! (*Regrouping, calmer.*) *Yes*. (*Totally calm.*) Yes.

*But despite her attempt at cool, she is now, for the first time,
showing true emotion, in the form of the smile pasted across
her face.*

I found my fucking note!

*She sits on the edge of the bed and unfolds the note. She
looks at the paper. Beat. And reads.*

'Dear Molly, when you read this, you will be thirty-nine and
your life will be very different than it is right now. You will
be older. You will have children, a husband and a fully-
rounded life. You will be smarter, or at least smart – unless
you've had a brain accident or somehow else become
retarded. I hope not, for your sake. When you read this, you
will not be a stutterer. I am sure. Right now I am a stutterer
and I hate it. But I am not stuttering as I write this. And you
will not stutter when you read it, because you will be braver.
I am not brave now because I am fourteen. But when you
read this at age thirty-nine you won't be scared and you
won't stutter. You will instead be happy. And things will
make sense. Or maybe not. Maybe this will make you want
to commit suicide. I hope not. I wish that you could write me
back to let me know what you are now. Hopefully you're
normal, happy, non-stuttering and your kids don't hate you. I
am going to try incredibly hard to make this happen.
Because I love you very much, Molly. And I want you to be
happy. Are you?'

MOLLY *sits quite still a moment. She just sits there, staring
straight ahead. And then she turns the paper over.*

And then I turn it over – and read – in someone else's
writing: 'Dear Molly. No.'

*Her face absorbs this. Silence. After several long moments,
she stands, placing the note in her pocket…*

I walk back upstairs, heading vaguely for the bathroom.
What I will do is climb back out the window; and leave. I'll
take the note with me, for better or worse, and I'll go back

through Maryland, to Washington, back to CNN and Jeff and
the occasional amicable lunch with Chuck and the several
pairs of shoes I took from my mother's closet after she died
– and that will be that. Or that will be –

RAY. Excuse me.

*MOLLY nearly gasps. RAY has stood from his stool and is
addressing her directly. Beat.*

MOLLY. What… who are you?

RAY. Who are *you*?

MOLLY. My name is, is Molly.

RAY. What're you doing here?

MOLLY.…I was looking for something.

RAY. Looking for what?

MOLLY. Something I thought I left here.

RAY. Did you break the window?

MOLLY. No.

RAY looks toward the 'window'.

RAY. That's funny, 'cause I got a call saying that a woman was
walking around this house; and that they heard the sound of
glass breaking; and that it was coming from the side of the
house.

MOLLY. Yes, I broke the window.

RAY. That's against the law.

MOLLY. I know. I'm sorry. Are you – ? What are you?

RAY. I'm the caretaker.

MOLLY. I see. I'm sorry. About the window. I really am.

Pause.

RAY. Okay.

MOLLY. I'm sorry –

RAY. You can't just go around breaking fucking windows.

MOLLY (*a bit taken aback*). You're right. I'm sorry. It was completely dumb of me. I just, I really needed to find something. I can pay for it. I can give you cash right now.

RAY. Okay.

MOLLY *wasn't expecting this.*

MOLLY. Ah, how much?

RAY. Eighty bucks.

MOLLY. Really? I mean, it's a pretty small window.

RAY. It's frosted glass.

MOLLY. Right. Okay…

She takes her wallet from her purse, takes out cash, hands it to him.

I only have sixty.

RAY. That's fine.

MOLLY *just stands there, watching him, almost studying him.*

MOLLY. So I should go.

RAY. Okay.

MOLLY. I have friends; waiting for me.

RAY. Where?

MOLLY. They dropped me off. But they know I'm here.

RAY (*a nod*). I see.

MOLLY *stands, still looking, almost squinting, at him.*

MOLLY. Okay.

RAY. Okay.

MOLLY *starts to move – needing to pass him in order to get out; he stays very still, not making it particularly easy for her.*

MOLLY. Excuse me.

RAY. Sure.

But he doesn't move that much.

MOLLY. Can you – I just need to –

RAY. Okay.

But he only moves a little. Finally and carefully MOLLY *gets past him. She is about to leave when –*

You live around here?

MOLLY. I'm sorry?

RAY. Do you live around here?

MOLLY. No.

RAY. What were you looking for?

MOLLY. Just something I left here.

RAY. When?

MOLLY. A while back.

RAY. What was it?

MOLLY. A hat.

RAY. How long ago?

MOLLY. Last summer.

RAY *nods.*

Thank you for not… being too mad.

RAY. You don't have to climb out the bathroom.

MOLLY. Oh?

RAY. I came in the front, so it's open.

MOLLY. Thank you.

RAY. Where are you meeting your friends?

MOLLY. Nearby. At the McDonald's.

RAY. Not back in DC?

MOLLY. No.

RAY. I saw your license plate.

MOLLY. Yeah, no. They're here. At the... *local* McDonald's. (*Looking at him.*) Are you – ? Do you *live* around here?

RAY. Yeah.

MOLLY (*still regarding him intently*). Is your name – may I ask your name?

RAY. Why?

MOLLY. I'm just curious.

RAY. It's Ray.

> MOLLY *takes this in…*

MOLLY. Really?

RAY. Yeah.

MOLLY. …Have you *always* lived here? Ray?

RAY. Not always, no.

MOLLY. Did you grow up here?

RAY. Nearby.

> *Pause.*

MOLLY. This is gonna sound weird, but... have we... have we *met*?

RAY. Beyond right now?

MOLLY. Yeah.

RAY. I don't think so.

MOLLY. My name is Molly. My family used to rent this house
and I feel like... like you and I might have met back then.

RAY. When?

MOLLY. In the eighties. The mid-eighties.

Beat, as RAY *looks at her.*

RAY. You think?

MOLLY. I do; yeah. I think.

RAY. How would we have met?

MOLLY. On the boardwalk. Randomly. Up at Rehoboth Beach.

RAY. ...Doubtful.

MOLLY. I think we did. Your name was Ray. And I kind of
recognise your – your face. (*Beat.*) I actually think we
might've hung out on a lifeguard stand; as the sun went
down; about twenty-four years ago, at dusk? Does that – ?

RAY. ...Not really.

MOLLY (*just looking at him*). Could your mom have been, like,
a real-estate agent?

RAY. No.

MOLLY. What'd she do?

RAY. She was a broker.

MOLLY. A *real-estate* broker?

RAY. She helped rent out summer rentals, sometimes.

MOLLY. *Okay!* – that's what I mean, she wasn't a *stock*broker.

RAY. No –

MOLLY. She was like a *real-estate* broker –

RAY. Yeah –

MOLLY. Or *agent* –

RAY. I guess –

MOLLY. You don't remember me – ?!

RAY. I'm not sure.

MOLLY. I was fifteen, you were, I think, sixteen.

No response.

I think we actually might've kissed; and hung out, on the lifeguard stand, with the sun going down behind us so we were just sort of watching as the water became... dark.

RAY *just stands there, perhaps recognising an image, perhaps not.*

RAY. Maybe.

MOLLY. *Thank you.*

Long beat as they regard each other, MOLLY *perhaps nodding slowly... and then, happier:*

So. What are you – like, *how're you doin'*, Ray?

RAY. I'm doing good.

MOLLY. Yeah?

RAY. Yeah.

MOLLY. Are you – life's treating you well?

RAY. Yeah. (*Pause*.) And you?

MOLLY. It's great, life's going great.

RAY. You live in Washington?

MOLLY. I live in DC, I work for CNN, great job, very busy, as I'm sure you can imagine, but I love it, I really do, so...

RAY. Are you, like, an anchor... person?

MOLLY. No, no, not me, I'm in communications, in the PR department. We call it the Puerto Rican department but that's kinda bigoted, so...

RAY. I see.

MOLLY. And you?

RAY. Umm, well, I still live around –

MOLLY. Right –

RAY. I do some caretaking, of the summer houses during the off-season, and I guess during the summer, too, if people need, whatever –

MOLLY. Absolutely.

RAY. I also have a little landscaping business.

MOLLY. Really?

RAY. Yeah, nothing big, pretty much just me, so –

MOLLY. Is that, is it *lawn-mowing* stuff – ?

RAY.…Some lawn mowing; sometimes just, you know, prettifying the area around the house, planting flowers. People like things to look kinda fancy these days.

MOLLY. *'Prettyfying'?*

RAY. Yeah.

MOLLY. Great word, I never, I rarely hear that.

RAY. I mighta made it up.

MOLLY. No, it's a word, I believe, absolutely.

> RAY *just looks at her…*

> *So* – you have the landscape business, you caretake, what else, are you married? Kids?

RAY. Divorced. One kid, a son, almost ten.

MOLLY. Oh, that's great. Not the divorce, but the son –

RAY. Yeah, thank you. I don't see him enough, but…

MOLLY. You should; fathers should see their sons.

RAY. I agree –

MOLLY. Does he not live around here?

RAY. No, they're in Florida, so…

MOLLY. I see.

Pause.

RAY. *You* married?

MOLLY. No. No. I was, ah, I was married, to a guy named Chuck, until about three years ago, and then… you know – (*Making a universal hand gesture for divorce.*)

RAY. Gotcha.

MOLLY. But it was a good marriage. No kids but a fine marriage.

RAY. Why did you guys break up?

MOLLY. I guess one could say that Chuck was a dick, or cocksucker, or… yeah, a dick. Still is. At his core. (*Beat.*) Not cocksucker *literally*, but we just didn't get along. At the end of the day, at 'dusk' – (*Nervous laugh.*) I just mean – at the end of the day we just didn't… *click*.

RAY. Okay.

As MOLLY lingers by the door.

MOLLY. It's so odd, I have such a… distinct memory of us meeting. (*Pause.*) We met at a pizza place on the boardwalk; I was buying lemonade and you were like, 'You're not gonna get a slice also?' and we just started talking. (*Pause.*) And we ended up on the lifeguard chair for – three hours? – talking and kissing. It's really – (*Tapping her brain.*) it's like indelible. (*Pause.*) Anyway.

RAY. It's true, I like pizza.

MOLLY. You do?

RAY. Yeah.

Awkward beat – MOLLY *feels she should go… but…*

MOLLY. I remember you told me you were planning to become a doctor. A heart surgeon, which sort of bowled me over, because it was so ambitious and, and *noble*. At least your *reasoning* was, because most doctors are more in it for the, you know, the Ferrari or the machismo or, you know, pussy, they're in it for pussy – sorry, I get potty mouth when I'm nervous, or I guess *pussy* mouth, so – I'm not usually… (*Pause.*) By the way I don't mean to imply that landscaping isn't noble, or ambitious, if that sounded crass, I just meant I remember how blown away I was by the heart-surgeon thing, especially at that age. (*Pause.*) Does any of that ring a – ?

RAY. Yeah.

MOLLY. Which part?

RAY. The heart-surgeon part.

MOLLY. You *did* wanna be a heart surgeon?

RAY. Yeah.

MOLLY (*a smile*). Wow.

RAY. I didn't succeed.

MOLLY. No, Ray, that's not what I –

RAY. I know, I was just kidding –

MOLLY. Oh –

RAY. I became a brain surgeon.

MOLLY. Really – ?

RAY. No. I didn't become anything.

MOLLY. That's not true, you have your own business –

RAY. True –

MOLLY. Which not everyone can say, I mean *I, I* work for a guy named *Jeff*, so…

Pause.

RAY. Were you really looking for your hat? Just now?

MOLLY.... Yes.

RAY. You were here last summer?

MOLLY. Yeah; funnily enough, my friends rented this house *last* summer, complete coincidence, and I came out for a weekend, and I left my favorite beach hat, so I finally had a Saturday off where I could drive out and... and look for it.

RAY. And it wasn't here?

MOLLY. No, why – do you have it?

RAY. No.

MOLLY. Oh – (*A laugh.*)... Anyway, I should go.

RAY. Do you wanna get a coffee?

Beat, as MOLLY *regards him.*

MOLLY. Right now?

RAY. Yeah. We could go to McDonald's. With your friends.

MOLLY *smiles, looks at her watch, thinks...*

MOLLY. I'm not sure I have time, Ray.

RAY. It's already made. All you have to do is order.

No answer.

Or not.

MOLLY. No, it's not that I'm *against* it, I just...

RAY. Maybe another time.

MOLLY. Absolutely.

They stand there a beat... before MOLLY *turns out and speaks to audience.*

And so we go for coffee. Not McDonald's. Denny's, because that's what he suggests. And we sit and order coffee. And I look at this guy, and I realise that the only reason I'm doing

this is because… is because that day we kissed on that
lifeguard chair, was… fucking fantastic. Not because he was
a great kisser, in fact I doubt he was, but because it was
maybe the last time in my life that… well, I'm not gonna say
that, but… It was the summer *after* I wrote myself the note,
meaning after I'd stopped stuttering; and the summer *before*
I started… gearing up to rampantly screw… Basically it was
the summer I was at my best.

Pause.

(*Quieter.*) This guy kissing me. Our lips learning how to be
truly tender for probably the first time ever for each of us; like
the first time you kiss someone with *finesse*. I even 'confessed'
to him that I'd been a stutterer. And what he said to me was…
he didn't actually say anything. I kid you not, he just turned to
me, and took my head in both his hands – (*Showing how.*) like
this – and he kissed me on the forehead… (*Reliving it,
perhaps fighting emotion, near whisper.*) so *intensely tenderly*.
And *then* he said, 'Molly. You've got it made.' (*Beat; barely
audible.*) And I believed him. I really thought… I had it made.
For the rest of my little life.

RAY. I actually *do* remember her. It just takes a while, when
you haven't thought of something in a lotta years. But the
lifeguard chair thing helps. (*Pause.*) The girl with the syrup
lips. Which I wouldn't have connected her to. Not to *those*
lips… not with a hundred guesses. Even now as she's telling
me. Not that she's not… It's just that you hold these things in
your head, and maybe every ten years or so they re-surface:
kissing a girl with syrup lips, at the end of a long day, on a
lifeguard stand. And you think, well man, isn't that just… an
over-romanticised little thing – that you're not even sure is
real. And then you move on. (*Beat.*) It's funny 'cause when I
remember that day now, as *she* comes into focus, from out of
this almost *floating* brain picture of syrup lips, I know that
the *reason* it's just an image, and not a full memory, is
because afterwards I got really ashamed. (*Pause.*) Because I
thought I'd pissed her off. Because all the time we were
kissing I was trying to stick my hands up her shirt. Which

she wouldn't let me do. And so for a while I just squeezed her, I guess you would say her half-formed breasts, from outside her shirt. And then I gave up on the breasts and tried to go down her pants, and she still wouldn't let me. I think I probably tried like seventeen times to get inside her shorts while we were up there, but she was pretty firm against it. It was almost like, as much as I was enjoying the kissing, it wasn't gonna be enough. Like I needed more because... because that's what I thought I needed. (*Pause.*) And I remember thinking after, 'God, she must've *hated* me for trying to get down her pants seventeen times.' I was totally... *embarrassed*, even as I walked her home later. (*Pause.*) But then I thought, 'Well, I'm a guy, so... I guess that's what we do. *She* understands.' And I sorta let it go. (*Pause.*) I don't think I've even *thought* about that since it happened. Even though I sometimes remember the lips.

RAY *and* MOLLY *sit at Denny's.*

I guess you could say the coffee here's not as good as McDonald's.

MOLLY. I think you could call it a toss-up, Ray.

RAY. You don't like McDonald's coffee?

MOLLY. I haven't had it since I was, like, six.

RAY. C'mon, I have a friend who *only* drinks McDonald's coffee. And that includes Starbucks.

MOLLY. How come *we* didn't go to Starbucks?

RAY. It's like three miles down the road.

She waits for more.

I was gonna suggest it, but...

MOLLY. So then how come we didn't go to McDonald's?

RAY. I was gonna suggest that too but I didn't wanna make you feel torn between sitting with me or with your friends.

MOLLY....My friends aren't really at McDonald's.

RAY. I know. What I mean is that I didn't want you to have to
keep lying.

MOLLY. Thoughtful of you.

RAY. I also thought you might think it was, you know –

MOLLY. Beneath me?

RAY. Yeah.

MOLLY. It is, Ray. McDonald's is beneath me.

RAY. It shouldn't be.

MOLLY. I know, I know. But it is.

Beat.

RAY. So you're driving back to DC?

MOLLY. Yeah.

RAY. What does someone like you do on a Saturday night in
DC?

MOLLY. ...I go out with friends.

RAY. Where do you go?

MOLLY. Dinner. Movies. Plays... Poetry slams.

RAY. Really?

MOLLY. No. But I'm very active.

RAY. I can imagine.

MOLLY. What does that mean?

RAY. Nothing, I can just imagine; that you would be an active
person. Instead of, like, a cat person.

MOLLY. I'm not a cat person, Ray.

RAY. Me neither.

MOLLY. What do *you* do on a Saturday night?

RAY. Well, I'm fairly calm... I'm on a bowling team.

MOLLY. *Are* you?

RAY. You don't bowl?

MOLLY. No. That's like the McDonald's of sports for me, so...

RAY. You should try it.

MOLLY. It's true, I'm being a snob. I should try it.

They sit in silence a moment...

So I have a long drive back.

RAY. You know... the more I'm sitting here looking at you, the more I'm... remembering. Like I remember, I *think*, that you told me you'd been a stutterer.

MOLLY. ...I did?

RAY. I think. And I just thought... it was really unexpected, that you said that. Because you seemed really confident.

MOLLY. As opposed to a sad and lonely cat person?

RAY. I guess. (*Beat.*) Did I – at the very end that day... Did I give you my address?

This catches her slightly off guard.

MOLLY. I don't think so.

RAY. I think I did.

MOLLY. ...Did we end up writing?

RAY. No.

MOLLY. Yeah, no, I don't recall any letters.

RAY. No, you never wrote. I think I gave you my address –

MOLLY. You didn't give me your address, Ray –

RAY. Yeah I did. It's not a big deal; but I do think I gave you my address – and then never heard from you again.

MOLLY. ...It's possible, but... I probably would have written.

RAY. Why?

MOLLY. Because I quite enjoyed our kiss.

RAY.…Me too. (*Pause*.) From what I can remember.

They watch each other an instant, and then:

MOLLY. Okay, I should really go.

She stands abruptly, reaching into her purse for money.

RAY. I got it –

MOLLY. No, it's okay –

RAY. Seriously, don't even think about it –

MOLLY. I work for CNN –

RAY. I know, but you also gave me sixty bucks for the window.

MOLLY. That's true –

RAY. In fact – (*Reaching into his pocket*.) I have no idea why I even took that, it was dumb –

MOLLY. No, no – I broke the window, take the money –

RAY. I can get it fixed for cheap, I was just being a jerk –

MOLLY. No you weren't –

RAY. I was, I was totally being a jerk – here –

He holds it out insistently… and finally she accepts.

MOLLY. Thank you.

RAY. No problem.

MOLLY. You're a nice guy, Ray.

RAY. You too, Molly. You're really sweet.

MOLLY. Thank you.

RAY. You're welcome.

MOLLY. It was really nice to see you again.

RAY. You too. You seem well.

MOLLY. Thank you.

RAY. Are you?

MOLLY. Am I – ?

RAY. You know – well?… Happy?

MOLLY.…Absolutely.

RAY. Good. You should be.

MOLLY. Thank you. Ray. (*Pause.*) Okay.

RAY. Okay. (*Beat.*) Molly?

MOLLY. Yeah?

RAY (*quiet, awkward*). Would it be weird if I… if I gave you a little kiss goodbye? (*Pause.*) For old time's sake?

MOLLY.…Seriously?

RAY. We don't have to.

MOLLY. No, I know; we don't. (*Beat.*) Okay.

RAY *hesitates… and then slowly, gently, kisses her once on the lips, perhaps lasting a couple beats longer than a little peck; he then looks at her…*

RAY. If I was a heart surgeon I'd maybe ask you out for dinner. (*Pause.*) But you should get back.

MOLLY *just stands there.*

You seem to be a really exquisite person, Molly. (*Slow, quiet.*) And I just wanna say that… that I now *definitely* remember our kiss. (*Pause; almost shy.*) It was really… innovative. For me. For like the first time. (*Pause.*) I don't think… I definitely didn't have that kind of thing; for a really long time after that.

MOLLY *takes this in, a smile… beat, and then:*

MOLLY. My junior year at Amherst, I dated a boy named Morris for three months and we didn't kiss *once*. (*Pause.*)

It was an experimental phase for me. But for some reason, I was more at peace with myself *then* than I have been since. So I know what you mean. Certain things… are hard to recapture. (*Beat.*) Where'd *you* go? Or, I mean, *did* you go?

RAY. To college?

MOLLY. Yeah.

RAY. No.

MOLLY. Obviously, not everyone does.

RAY. I mean, I actually have about half the necessary credits.

MOLLY. Did you drop out?

RAY. Kind of.

MOLLY.…Kind of what?

RAY. Yeah. I went, but only for a while.

MOLLY. So where did you go? – for a while?

RAY. By correspondence. And then some community college.

MOLLY. Cool.

Awkward beat.

RAY. I was in prison.

MOLLY. Oh. (*Pause.*) For a long time?

RAY. Ten years.

MOLLY *nods. Beat.*

MOLLY. For what?

Beat.

RAY. I was part of this thing where a guy got killed; murdered; during a fight.

MOLLY. *Murdered?*

RAY. Yeah.

MOLLY....Did *you* – ?

RAY. No. But I was there. And I didn't do enough to stop it.

MOLLY nods a little. She perhaps picks up her purse; then stops. Pause.

MOLLY (*polite*). Who was the guy? Who was murdered?

RAY. It was a student who was here at the beach one summer.

MOLLY....Wow.

Beat.

RAY. He was actually a gay student. (*Pause.*) Just to...

MOLLY just looks at him, attempting to fathom.

MOLLY. *What?*

RAY. I was part of a murder that was committed against a gay kid; a gay man.

MOLLY....When?

RAY. When I was eighteen.

Beat.

MOLLY. How old were you when you and I met?

RAY. I must've been sixteen.

MOLLY is still just looking at him.

You should –

MOLLY. You're serious?

RAY. Yeah.

MOLLY....Jesus.

They stand in silence a moment.

I'm sorry – but... can I... do you mind if I ask what happened?

RAY. Sure.

MOLLY. You were with a guy who murdered a gay college student?

RAY. Hmm hmm.

MOLLY. And did you... *help*?

RAY (*calm*). In the sense that me and this other guy didn't do enough to stop it.

MOLLY (*neutral*). There were three of you?

RAY *nods*.

And you didn't try to... to stop him?

RAY. I did. But... not enough.

MOLLY. Why not?

RAY. I don't know.

MOLLY. What do you mean – ?

RAY. I would say I have a *lot* of answers.

MOLLY. So... then – why're you saying you don't know?

RAY. Because I'm not sure if they're right.

MOLLY. I see. (*Beat.*) But you knew he was gay?

RAY. Yeah.

MOLLY. Did you call the police?

RAY. After.

MOLLY. How long after?

RAY. Twenty-five minutes.

MOLLY.... *Why?*

RAY. I don't know.

MOLLY. Can you stop saying that?

RAY *says nothing*.

I'm sorry – I'm just – the three of you sat there with a dead body for twenty-five minutes?

RAY. No; we had left when the beating stopped.

Pause.

MOLLY. To do what?

RAY.... We ate pizza.

MOLLY *absorbs...*

MOLLY.... Oh. Wow.

Beat. She gathers her stuff.

(*Neutral.*) It was nice to see you again, Ray. Good luck with the caretaking.

RAY. Bye.

And MOLLY *leaves.*

MOLLY. And I drive back to DC. I don't know what to say. I'm speechless. (*Beat.*) I take that back. (*Pause.*) I am a person who understands life. In fact, I am in a profession where the *explication* of certain of life's complexities, social trends and political machinations are, are what I get paid for. And so I 'get' that people had shitty childhoods, and that good people make grave mistakes and that boys will be boys and even that eighteen-year-olds in America, particularly in the late 1980s, were subject to cultural reinforcements and societal underpinnings and an overall *lack* of a moral compass. I *get* all that – and yet I cannot abide what I just heard. That I cannot abide. I can't 'tolerate' it, to use that insultingly polite word that poses as empathetic, and I *certainly* cannot accept it.

RAY. I don't think I had what it took to be a heart surgeon anyway. Yes, it was a thought, maybe even an intention, at some point along the line, at least when I said it, but had what happened not happened, would I have really followed through? *Could* I have? I didn't have the grades to get into a serious college, and even if I had, to get through four years and then into med school? And then into heart surgery? I work hard to be a realist. So to blame my lack of heart-surgery skills solely upon what happened – simply wouldn't be true.

MOLLY. And so I drive away. As fast as I can, back across the endless Bay Bridge, back to our Capitol and cosmopolitan city where people sip martinis and a black president works the elliptical and there's a Starbucks on every corner and people have college degrees and Barney Frank wields enormous and unyielding power. *With impunity*. Call me a snob.

RAY *and* MOLLY *sit on bench.*

RAY. I guess I was just surprised.

MOLLY. That I called?

RAY. That I would ever see you again.

MOLLY. Why?

RAY. I don't make people very comfortable.

MOLLY. It's tough first-date material. (*Pause.*) I'm sorry, I don't mean to...

RAY. It's fine. (*Pause.*) So why *did* you call?

MOLLY. I felt dumb about leaving it the way I did with you. (*Pause.*) But I'm lucky I found your number. Your business should have a website.

RAY. Yeah, I gotta get on that.

MOLLY. True. (*Attempted humour.*) Don't wanna get left behind on the information highway, Ray.

They smile a little. Beat.

All that to say I guess I just wanted to, you know, say goodbye in a more proper fashion.

RAY. Gotcha.

Beat.

MOLLY. You had a good week?

RAY. Yeah, I did. (*Pause.*) And you?

MOLLY. Yep. Swamped at work these days, but...

RAY. But it's going well?

MOLLY. It's fine. I work for a guy named Jeff. He's fine.

RAY waits for more.

Not that Jeff and I are – (*A laugh.*) He's my boss, so...

RAY just looks at her. Beat.

So, are you a Redskins fan, Ray?

RAY. Ah, yeah. I guess I am.

MOLLY. Not very politically correct; their name.

RAY. No, I guess not.

MOLLY. But it's not like they're the only ones; the only team with a bigoted name.

Beat. She is regarding him...

RAY. So, was there more that you wanted to – ?

MOLLY. Yes.

Pause.

RAY. Was it that you were interested in how to become a caretaker?

MOLLY (*a small smile*). No. I mean... (*Pause.*) I guess I was just wondering if there was any way you could tell me more. About what happened.

Pause.

RAY (*half smile*). You wanna know how a guy you kissed when you were a teenager...

MOLLY. Yes. I suppose. (*Pause.*) Not that kissing someone a hundred years ago gives you huge insight into who that someone's gonna be, but...

RAY. But you're curious.

MOLLY. Yeah. I guess I'm curious. If you wanted to just talk about it a little more.

Beat.

RAY. Well. (*Pause.*) I was with these two friends of mine; and we had crashed a party of a bunch of college kids who were renting a house about a block from the beach, over in Rehoboth. And when they realised we weren't with their group they tried to kick us out. And we didn't wanna go but we were outnumbered so we finally did. Then my friends and I went and got drunk and came back to the house later that night; and we threw a rock at where we were pretty sure the guy was sleeping – the one who had kicked us out. And then he came out.

MOLLY. Was he the one who ended up getting killed?

RAY. Yeah. His name was Craig Sollins. And, ah, he came out, and we asked him why he'd kicked us out of the party and he just, he said it was because it had been private and he wanted to keep it that way. And my friend Bobby, Bob Millan, was really drunk and pissed and he just, I guess he didn't like the way Craig was answering the questions, and he just started punching him.

MOLLY.…Were there not other people in the house?

RAY. I guess there were two other guys inside at that point but they later said they'd slept through it; 'cause they were drunk.

MOLLY. Is that – true?

RAY. I don't know. It wasn't actually that loud, because once Craig came out it was actually a conversation for most of it, until Bob started punching.

Pause.

MOLLY. Did he… (*Quiet.*) So Craig was… *punched* to death?

RAY. Yeah.

Beat.

MOLLY. And were you…?

RAY. I was watching.

Beat. MOLLY *at a loss for what to say…*

MOLLY. I feel like this boardwalk hasn't changed for twenty-five years.

RAY doesn't answer. Silence.

Did you know Craig was gay?

RAY. Yeah. (*Pause.*) I could just tell. From when we were at the party earlier that night, it was a lotta gay guys, who were there. And I mean… it turned out to be right.

MOLLY *is just watching him.*

Molly?

MOLLY. Yeah.

RAY. I'm starting to feel a little weird about this.

MOLLY. Why?

RAY. Because I feel like… this is gonna make you despise me. And I don't really want that. (*Pause.*) I mean, is that why you called? To sort of –

MOLLY. No.

RAY. So then it's for some other reason?

MOLLY. Like a date?

RAY. No –

MOLLY. It's not a date, Ray.

RAY. I didn't say it was –

MOLLY. We're on a bench –

RAY. I know –

MOLLY. On the boardwalk –

RAY. I know –

MOLLY. I just –

RAY. You wanted to see if you could psychoanalyse me more than I've been able to do for myself?

Pause.

MOLLY. No. That's not what I'm trying to do. I just thought it would be… informative. For me.

RAY. Okay.

RAY *takes this in for what it is…*

Beat.

The punching lasted two or three minutes, with Bobby calling him a fag; and other stuff. And like I said the other day, at first I tried to stop it, which is when Bobby punched me, pretty hard in the head. And so then I backed off; until he was done. (*Pause.*) The other guy, his name was Tim Jenson, he told me to let it play out, and, so…

MOLLY. Did you not – didn't you know that what was happening was wrong?

RAY. Yeah. I did. I knew it was wrong.

Beat.

I'm not sure why you'd be wanting to be informed about this, Molly. Unless you're looking at it like a charity case. In which case –

MOLLY. I'm not. Doing that. Why would it be charity? I was just curious.

RAY. Okay. So you're done then? – With the curiosity?

Beat.

MOLLY (*not vindictive*). Can I just ask why you didn't do more to stop it?

RAY. Because I froze.

MOLLY.…Is it something you'd done before?

RAY. Yeah.

MOLLY. When?

RAY. Always.

MOLLY. You always froze?

RAY. Yeah. Or, like, hid. As a kid, and, obviously, as a teenager, when things became… chaotic, or just too much, I would always try to escape.

MOLLY. Why?

RAY. I just didn't like confronting – things… And I think that over the years, as I kept doing it, I was able to *do* that – for bigger and bigger things. Like a skill; when at first you do it on a small level, and as you get better you can do it for bigger and bigger things.

MOLLY (*almost an aside*). Well, that's very… concise.

RAY. Which is why I'd rather say I don't know.

MOLLY. Instead of blaming it on a deficient childhood.

RAY. Yeah –

MOLLY. Was that the case with you?

RAY. Hard to say.

MOLLY. No one taught you to 'hate homosexuals'?

RAY.…Not overtly. (*Beat*.) There are programmes, in prison, where they teach you to try not to be vulnerable to those types of… excuses.

MOLLY. See – that's informative.

RAY.…There's this one called restorative justice, which is about offender accountability, violence prevention, victim restoration; and then community involvement –

MOLLY. *Victim* restoration?

RAY. Yeah.

Pause.

MOLLY. How does one restore a dead victim, Ray?

RAY. You don't.

MOLLY. I mean, I don't know if you've had friends who were gay-bashed. *Have* you?

RAY. No –

MOLLY. Well, if you did it would be more… evident that you can't just take a course and have the whole thing go away. That the lives that are lost and the messages that are sent –

RAY. I'm not saying it goes away, I'm saying that there's work you *can* do, on your end, to, to trace the steps you took to where you were able to commit a violent act.

Pause. MOLLY *waits for more.*

To identify things you didn't *realise* were violent, like the first time you *witnessed* violence, and how that led to *permitting* it, and then to calling someone a fag – anything that you maybe never realised was assaultive, so that you –

MOLLY. Gotcha.

RAY *looks at her; she tries to stay polite.*

No. I understand. Thank you.

RAY. You think I'm… that I'm just talking jargon?

MOLLY. I think that's how it's coming out.

RAY. Well, it *is* jargon – unless you've been part of an actual murder situation, in which case you have a more open mind.

MOLLY. Believe me, Ray, I'm trying to have an open mind –

RAY. Good, because the thing is it *is* possible to have mean-ingful restoration, within the framework of governmental or community action. So that you're part of a programme that's itself part of –

MOLLY. Okay, but do *you* work in one of those programmes?

RAY. No.

MOLLY. So then what *do* you do, Ray, besides talk about how you're no longer a homophobe?

RAY. You know what, you're being a fucking jerk.

There's just enough edge on this to freeze her for a beat...

MOLLY. Well, that's nice. (*Beat... neutral.*) Do you know what time it is?

RAY. No.

MOLLY. You don't wear a watch?

RAY shakes his head.

Me neither. (*Pause.*) For me, that's rebellion. (*Pause.*) Jeff calls it irresponsible.

She looks at him, perhaps hoping to have broken the tension a bit; it hasn't. Beat.

This is making me...

They sit in silence for a long moment.

Last year, when things were insane at work, my mom was living down in Williamsburg; and her friend called to say she was in the hospital because she'd had a stroke, and so I called to find out what was up and my mom was like, 'It's okay, Molly, don't come down, it's just a mild stroke, I'm fine.' (*Pause.*) And so I didn't. I mean, I said I'd come the next day, which was a Saturday. (*Pause.*) Needless to say she died that night.

RAY. How?

MOLLY. The stroke had caused a clot; that the doctors missed seeing.

Beat.

RAY. Well. So maybe you should've gone down. (*Pause.*) One lives and learns.

MOLLY looks at him...

MOLLY. The last thing I said to her was, 'Watch CNN tonight, we have a great interview with Timothy Geithner.' (*Looks at him*.) Last thing I said to my mother before she died. (*Pause*.) Talk about frozen.

Beat.

You don't have a girlfriend, Ray?

RAY *shakes his head*.

But do you function? Are you a functioning person? Not professionally but personally; do you – are you *happy*?

RAY. I'm all right.

MOLLY. Do you have friends? Beside your bowling… mates?

RAY. Some. (*Pause*.) I take care of my mom now, so I spend a lot of time with her. She lives around here.

MOLLY. Do you have any gay friends?

RAY.…Not really. One, kinda. A guy at the hardware store; go figure; but we're just friendly; I wouldn't say 'friends'.

MOLLY. So he doesn't know about your – ?

RAY (*shakes his head*). I mean, where would I even start?

MOLLY.…Do you still drink?

RAY.…Not really. In prison, you know, you really can't drink much.

MOLLY. You mean it's not like on TV where everyone's always drinking 'toilet hooch'?

RAY. Well, yeah, there's hooch, not toilet hooch, but there's definitely, you know, homemade wine, or whatever –

MOLLY. Did you used to drink it?

RAY. I tried it a couple times. It's pretty fucking gross.

MOLLY. What's it made of?

RAY. It's mostly just fruit and sugar that's been fermented; under someone's bed. I wouldn't recommend it.

MOLLY *watches him, taking him in…*

MOLLY. What was prison like?

RAY.…If you're smart about it you can pretty much stay out of the way of the bad stuff. (*Beat.*) Is this the part where you get to know the soft underbelly of the hardened criminal?

MOLLY (*perhaps a small smile*). No.

RAY. It's just more curiosity?

MOLLY. Yes. It's curiosity.

Silence. Beat.

Was ten years considered a lot? For that crime?

RAY. I dunno. I probably could've cooperated more. They tried me before Bobby so they gave me a chance to testify as to his motives.

MOLLY. Meaning – ?

RAY. They wanted me to say if I thought he had specifically gone back to Craig's house in order to kill him, or even just beat him up, *because* he was gay.

MOLLY. And did you?

RAY. No.

MOLLY. Why not?

RAY. Because I wasn't sure it was true. I mean, it's true we went back because a part of us was pissed off that we'd been kicked out by these gay guys, so –

MOLLY. Well, then doesn't that speak to motive – ?

RAY. It speaks to why we went back there but not what we went back to *do*. None of us ever said, 'Let's go back and kill that gay kid.'

MOLLY *doesn't love this answer but no longer wants to express anger.*

MOLLY. But –

RAY. When I testified, all I did was not say more than I *knew*.
Which I'm sure was partially loyalty to Bobby but was also
me not thinking I could get inside his head. I'm still trying to
understand what was in *my* head, so –

MOLLY. Fine, it's just that the thing with hate crimes, Ray, is that
you *do* have to get inside the person's head, based on the *outer*
evidence they're giving you. People are targeted *every day*
because of who they are, meaning there's a *reason* those hate-
crime laws exist and thus you can't just sit there and say that a
fucking *bigot's* reasoning is 'beyond' you, because they
frankly tend not to be that smart. (*Pause.*) Forgive my passion.

Beat.

Can I ask you something?

RAY *nods, perhaps a resigned smile.*

The part of you that turned away that night. Do you think it's
still...?

RAY *takes this in, watching her.*

RAY. I would hope not. (*Pause.*) But... it's hard to say.

They let this sit.

You're trying to ask if I'm 'fully rehabilitated'?

MOLLY. I don't know *what* I'm trying to ask.

RAY (*not harsh*). Too bad there isn't one of those tests where
you can, like, add water to see if I float or something, to
know whether I'm all fixed up.

MOLLY. It would certainly be... helpful, in terms of your
flotation-device capability.

Beat.

RAY. One of the parts of this programme is a Victim Empathy
thing, where you can write a letter to your victim, or, actually
what *I* did, was I wrote a letter to Craig's parents. Which I
sent.

MOLLY. What'd it say?

RAY. Well… it said I was sorry. I mean, what else can you…
but, also, for *me*, it was rehabilitative, because it made me
think about the stuff I'd been taught over the years, and how
I hadn't seen that that was bad teaching; *incorrect* teaching;
and then how I'd made choices *based* on that. (*Pause.*) The
programmes teach you that part of being human is not being
human *enough*; that our lives are about, you know… trying
to step into our *full* humanity, so that we're better at
recognising someone *else's*. Which is what *I* definitely
lacked. (*Pause; quieter; less polished.*) I know that part of
why I didn't fully see Craig was because I knew he was gay.
It was like I was looking at him with blinders on. (*Pause.*)
But I didn't write all that in my letter. I basically just said I
was sorry, to his mom and dad.

MOLLY. Did they write you back?

RAY. No.

Beat.

MOLLY. Do you still have *your* dad?

RAY. No.

Beat.

Can I ask *you* something?

MOLLY. Sure.

RAY. When you came back to that house the other day. Were
you *actually* looking for a hat?

MOLLY. No. I was looking for a letter. That I'd written to
myself, from when I was a kid.

RAY. Why?

MOLLY. It was like a message. And I was just trying to
remember what it said.

RAY. …Did you find it?

MOLLY. Yeah.

RAY. What'd it say?

MOLLY. It said to have more confidence.

RAY. You don't have confidence?

MOLLY. I'm okay.

RAY....Do you have a boyfriend?

MOLLY. Why, is that a sign of confidence?

RAY. I suppose it's either confidence or desperation, depending on who you choose.

MOLLY. I agree. (*Pause*.) No. No boyfriend.

RAY. But you function? You're a functioning person?

> MOLLY *just looks at him, and then:*

MOLLY. Yes, thank you.

RAY. Did your stuttering ever come back?

MOLLY. No.

RAY. Well, there you go, *that's* good.

MOLLY. Yep. (*Beat*.) My shrink says I stutter inside. (*An awkward little laugh*.) I'm kidding. (*Pause*.) Actually, coming back here and running in to *you*... was interesting, because my one memory of you is of being very fully... alive. Which I only know because in the years *after* I met you it was like I stepped *away* from... my 'humaness'.

RAY. Why?

MOLLY. Well, it's certainly not something I did on purpose. I think... it's hard; to live correctly. And, so... Yeah.

> *Beat*.

RAY. Did you pick to meet at this bench because it felt safe?

MOLLY. Yes.

RAY. Were you scared to actually spend time – ?

MOLLY. I didn't wanna indicate that this was gonna be 'intimate' time together –

RAY. No, I get that –

MOLLY. But I agree, it's a little odd –

RAY. No, I was just wondering – if you *did*... wanna spend some intimate time together. Not... what I mean is at a restaurant. Would you like to have some dinner; with me? (*Pause*.) Seeing as we're both single.

MOLLY. I don't know, Ray.

RAY *turns to speak to audience*.

RAY. We go to this little Italian place I used to go to with my mom before my mom decided she didn't like the Italians any more. Not all Italians, just these ones, who she thinks tried to poison her with clam sauce. (*Beat*.) It's funny, 'cause I had wanted to call Molly after the first time I saw her but I didn't think I had a chance in hell once I'd told her my little story. There are certain people you can just tell about. Which is not to say I really know, because except for my ex-wife there aren't many women that I've been 'emotionally intimate' with who I've told. I mean, there haven't been that many women anyway, but... And my marriage was a situation where I got married almost right out of prison to a woman who, well, she's a nurse, so she's a caring person, a caretaker, if you will, so... Point is I had thought Molly a very sophisticated person who would view my crime as... irreconcilable with her world. (*Pause*.) Which is not to say there aren't sophisticated people out there who aren't 'curious' about people who have done things such as I. There are; they just, don't necessarily wanna sleep with you. (*Pause*.) What I mean is that for me, my sex life is gonna be with people to who I *don't* talk about my past; and my *love* life is gonna be with, you know... nurses.

So I hadn't called. And when *she* called, I figured she was just curious... anthropologically. Until she told me about that letter she'd written to herself.

I dunno. But there was something there that made me think, 'Well, maybe here is that very rare, basically nonexistent someone to whom I could both speak honestly about my own stupid life... and *with* whom – I also might get to sleep; with. (*Pause.*) And so I took her to the Italian place.

RAY *and* MOLLY *at a restaurant.*

MOLLY. I'm assuming you realise you're not gonna be able to sleep with me just because you're taking me out for dinner.

RAY....Who said I'm taking you out for dinner?

MOLLY. Fair enough.

RAY. I'm kidding –

MOLLY. You sure? – I mean these pasta entrées are *nine bucks a pop.*

RAY. Order whatever you want. (*Reading the menu.*) Although you might wanna try the clams.

MOLLY. Really?

RAY. I'm kidding. I mean, they're fine, but...

They study their menus.

MOLLY. You've been here a lot?

RAY. Yeah. I bring my mom here sometimes.

MOLLY. It's nice.

RAY. It's okay. (*Beat.*) Are you regretting that you said yes to coming?

MOLLY. No.

RAY. 'Cause you can leave, I'd understand.

MOLLY. No, I'm fine.

RAY....Do you like your job at CNN?

MOLLY. Yeah. It's fun; I also think I'm good at it. I mean DC's so *dumb*, it's like going to work in a jungle each morning in which the wild animals are the people trying to manage public opinion. And because everyone and their mom wants CNN on *their* side, it's exciting, because what it ends up being is a job of trying to micromanage the *image* that America shoots out to the world.

RAY. Wow.

MOLLY. But it's mostly stupid.

RAY. Why – ?

MOLLY. Because there are days you're just like, 'Why even attempt to articulate what is, at heart, a mostly chaotic mishmash of *shit* going on and people acting inexcusably due to insane *ideologies* that *we're* attempting to neatly and reductively label as "news".'

Pause.

RAY. It's funny about news. Like you say, it's obviously important to try to understand how the world works, but it's also wild how sometimes the whole thing just boils down to a second.

MOLLY. Sure.

Pause.

RAY. I saw this article the other day about the trial of a Khmer Rouge leader. And they had this whole parade of witnesses with missing limbs and memories of their loved ones getting killed and just the *horrible* shit that this man had permitted and done. And I guess at one point one of the witnesses was describing how the Khmer Rouge guy had basically allowed for the death of his wife. And yet somehow this witness had also been *saved* by this guy, because he was a violin player and the Khmer guy wanted someone to play the violin for him. And the witness and the Khmer leader had become friends, over the following years, despite one having essentially killed the other's wife. *Somehow* in the world they were living in, for that duration, they'd struck up a friendship. And in the intervening years they'd fallen out of touch – until the day that the violin player testified at the guy's trial. And when he took the stand, the Khmer guy looked at him and started crying, like apparently really genuinely, and said, 'I send my respects to the soul of your wife.' And... I dunno, maybe that's a dumb story. But it struck me because, talk about communication – to *me* that communicated so much about the humanity of these two guys who, if you look at it one way, had either had their humanity completely stripped from them, or, with the Khmer guy, didn't have almost *any* for a very long time, and now maybe does a little.

Beat.

MOLLY. See, that doesn't really – I'm not at all applying this to you, but that doesn't move me because it just seems like the Khmer guy wants to show the judge or the jury that he feels bad, and this is his way of doing it. Because if you want to communicate true remorse you don't wait until thirty years after the fact when you're in the middle of a trial for crimes against humanity.

RAY....Maybe you're right –

MOLLY. And I'm not saying that someone like *you*, for instance, can't be genuine in your remorse, over a single moment in your youth when you allowed yourself to look the other way and have subsequently spent what sounds like a large portion of your adulthood trying to make up for and understand it – so the two aren't equal, but it does seem that, like if I was covering that for CNN, I'd hold it up as an example of the artifice of contrition.

RAY. But what if it was genuine?

MOLLY. Well, then he'd need to back it up with a lot *more* contrition, *acts* of contrition, the making of amends, the, the, the necessary *reflection* that constitutes true and genuine forward-leaning development in terms of one's humanity, which goes a little to what *you* were saying earlier about becoming *more* human, every day, as we advance through our lives.

RAY. But... *you* haven't done that. I mean, didn't you say earlier that you've stepped *away from* your own humanity since you were younger?

MOLLY. Yes, but not by fucking *impaling little Cambodian babies on sword tips*!

RAY. Fine –

MOLLY. And it's not like I ever committed a crime against humanity in the first place, except maybe my *own*, which is my own business. Whereas with the Khmer Rouge we *can* stand in judgement –

RAY. I'm not saying we can't, and we do and should, I'm just saying that every now and then all it takes is a sentence from someone, or even just a look in their eyes, for us to *feel* the humanity inside even the most villainous of people. And that actually this Khmer Rouge guy, whether on purpose or not, managed to communicate, to me at least, in an unexpected way, something that felt actually *true*.

MOLLY. Why're you telling me this?

RAY. I just thought it was interesting.

MOLLY. Which part?

RAY. That you were talking about the chaos of the world and your attempts to try and explain it with some type of meaning, and that you work for a TV news channel that is on for every single second of every single day and yet when I watch it I rarely walk away feeling like I've understood a single fucking thing; and then I pick up the paper and read one sentence from one single horrific fucking man and I suddenly feel like I understand something; even if it's only for a split second. (*Pause.*) But then I try to verbalise it to *you* and I go right back to feeling like I don't know *any*thing.

MOLLY *regards him. Beat.*

MOLLY. Point taken.

RAY. I was kidding about the clams; don't get them; they're not good here.

MOLLY. You're feisty. I don't think I knew that about you. Doesn't really go with the whole 'calm' thing. (*Beat; a half smile.*) Does that come from being in jail?

RAY. Prison. Possibly.

Beat.

What's the worst thing *you* ever did?

MOLLY *just looks at him.*

I mean, you know *my* worst thing, so I was just wondering if you had anything bad you ever did. Not that it would be equal, but... (*Pause.*) Or even that just *happened* to you.

MOLLY. Nothing bad's *ever* happened to me, Ray... That's why I'm a fucking jerk.

RAY *takes this in. Beat.*

RAY. So then what's the worst thing you ever *did*?

MOLLY. I was a telemarketer one summer during college.

RAY *just looks at her.*

The worst thing... is that I never take risks.

RAY. In life?

MOLLY. Yeah.

RAY. *Never?*

MOLLY. Never. Not real ones. (*Pause.*) I think that's why I never wrote you; after that time we met when we were kids.

RAY....So you *do* remember taking my address?

MOLLY. Yeah. But I didn't wanna write because for me it was perfect; it was a perfect dusk. I was confident; not defensive; happy – and I didn't wanna screw it up.

RAY....You took a risk by calling me yesterday; to meet you on the bench.

MOLLY. That wasn't a risk... I came back to bury you.

RAY. But… you didn't. I mean – not yet.

MOLLY. True.

Beat.

RAY. What do you think happened? That made you stop.

MOLLY. Stop taking risks?

RAY. Yeah. I mean, was it suddenly; gradually; both?

Pause.

MOLLY. Probably the same as everyone else. Fear. Of not being written back to; not being *loved*. Pretty fucking quotidian, actually.

RAY. But there's nothing *specific* you can point to?

MOLLY. I think that emotional constipation is fairly specific.

RAY. I know but what *caused* it? Why're you working at CNN if what you really want is to be a poet?

MOLLY. Who said I wanted to be a poet?

RAY. I'm just saying –

MOLLY. I know, but why're you saying *that*?

RAY. I dunno – why – *do* you wanna be a poet?

MOLLY. Fuck no.

RAY. Fine, but do you wanna work at CNN?

MOLLY. No –

RAY. So why *are* you? Why not take a risk and do what you want? Did you like, hit your head on the jungle gym?

MOLLY *smiles. Beat.*

MOLLY *(simple)*. I guess it was just easier. Over time. To compromise.

RAY.… Well, you shouldn't.

MOLLY *looks at him, a small smile at his chivalry, and yet obviously touched. Beat.*

MOLLY. Do they not have waitresses here?

RAY (*a smile*). Yeah, it doesn't seem like it –

MOLLY. It's ridiculous –

RAY *turns and speaks to audience.*

RAY. I mentioned earlier that I have good memory for certain images. Which unfortunately holds true for the night that my friend Bobby beat Craig Sollins to death. (*Beat.*) The first is a sound image, of my voice, just before the punching started. Craig and Bobby were standing face to face, not even yelling, and Tim and I were behind Bobby, like an after-school special: we were the little henchmen, backing up this bully. And all of sudden, Bobby called Craig a fag. He goes, 'You know what, you're a big fucking fag.' And what *I* did was… I laughed. Out loud. When he said that. I laughed pretty loud. (*Pause.*) So there's that. Which I didn't talk about. With her. (*Beat.*) The second image is of the first punch. It came out of nowhere. They were talking and Bobby just punched the *shit* out of Craig; an incredibly jagged, surprise-attack punch that caught Craig somewhere between his mouth and nostril, mostly missing, actually, and which made in Craig's eyes this very distinct look of betrayal. He just… looked *completely* betrayed… Like everything had changed. (*Pause.*) The third is of after Bobby had jumped on him and continued punching. Specifically of one punch that hit dead-on and turned Craig's head to the side; and when his head came back around… his eyes weren't present; just weren't with us any more; even though he was still making these murmuring sounds. But what was clear was that he was going away; he was just going away; and he knew it; and I knew it too.

MOLLY *turns and speaks to audience.*

MOLLY. I go home with him that night; and we make the kind of love… that I really like to make. His little 'condominium' is way overheated so we're both really sweaty, hugely sweaty, and not just our foreheads; everywhere; I'm sweaty under my arms, between my tits, up inside my thighs; my – my *coccyx* is sweaty. It's phenomenal. The whole thing satiates my need for freakishness, because Ray is, Ray obviously has issues, like, I dunno, untapped reserves of violence that he maybe feels bad about never having tapped into. He's never threatening, he's just… wound like an exceedingly compressed coil, for a theoretically calm and repentant guy. It's like – I don't wanna be too, but – it's like he's fucking me with this innate sort of need to make a point that his life has not been a complete and utter waste. He's so needy and *inside* me, he's so hyper-intensely *inside* me that it's… that I start to cry. And I'm not a crier, I'm really not. (*Pause.*) And afterwards… this guy is touching my face like we're literally the last two people on the planet, and we've just discovered each other after decades of wandering the barren, nuclear-scorched earth alone… (*Pause.*) And all he wants to say is hello. (*Even quieter.*) He just wants to say hello.

RAY *resumes speaking to audience.*

RAY. Shame is toxic. They teach you that. One of the first things you learn in these programmes. Shame is toxic, and it will destroy the living human being inside you. And so sometimes we call it *de*toxification – this process of learning *not* to be ashamed; not only for what you've done, but for what *led* you to doing it – or in my case *not* doing it, in the first place. The shame of not thinking I was strong enough… to step in and stop it. It's really corrosive, because *that* shame probably still exists. The *initial* shame, that I wasn't enough of a man, to the point where I *laughed* to somehow affirm it – which is about as big a cliché as there is – *that* shame, no matter how much I voice it, address it, heal it, teach it; *that* shame, knowing that it led to what it led to – *that*… is hard to shake. (*Pause.*) The last image that is directly related to that night, is of the blood coming out of Craig Sollins' left ear. After Bobby stood up and the three of us started to walk away. I looked back, and I saw the blood trickling from his ear. And I knew, or at least I know now and I think I must have…

known back then, that that blood was indicative of the
internal bleeding that was rapidly taking place. So that image,
which is… potent enough on its own, is a million times
quadrupled by what it *means*. That image of blood from the
ear, and thus the overflow of blood on his brain, is quite
honestly, rarely farther away from my mind than right here.

*He is holding his fist right aside his head; he then slowly
lowers it… as he and* MOLLY *now sip coffee.*

MOLLY. What do you usually do for breakfast, Ray?

RAY. Cereal.

MOLLY. Cereal, huh? What kind?

RAY. Depends, I have several; what do you like?

MOLLY. I actually think *you* should choose. My ex-husband
and I used to fight about cereal.

RAY. How did you manage to do that?

MOLLY. Well, he was all into the very organic, flaxy, banana
fucking *nut* kind, whereas I often awake with a hankering for
ChocoDonuts.

RAY. That's… those aren't good for you, Molly.

MOLLY. Shut up, Ray, they're my only vice. Besides having
sex with convicted felons. *ChocoDonuts* remind me of my
childhood.

RAY. Oh. And what does having sex with convicted felons
remind you of?

MOLLY. My late teenage years… I'm kidding.

RAY. Did you not have a happy childhood?

MOLLY. I had a great childhood. Except for the stuttering. And
then the ensuing sexual misconduct.

RAY. You were sexually…?

MOLLY. Misconductive? Yes. Relatively. But not the summer I
met you. Like I said, that was my summer of… content.

RAY *kind of nods*.

RAY. Did you like coming out here, to the beaches?

MOLLY. I did, for the most part. It was always a very relaxing week; with my parents; kind of. (*Beat.*) Do you ever make it to DC?

RAY. I took my son there a couple years ago to see the monuments, which was great. (*Pause.*) I'm probably not really a city guy.

MOLLY. Well, you're not missing much. I mean, it's great, but, it's beautiful out here. Especially in the winter.

RAY. It's true, I love it off-season, incredibly quiet.

MOLLY. Yeah.

Beat.

RAY. You're really frickin' beautiful, Molly.

MOLLY (*a blush*). *Thank* you, Ray.

RAY. You're welcome.

MOLLY. You're pretty cute yourself.

RAY. I wouldn't say that.

MOLLY. I like it.

RAY. 'It'?

MOLLY. Your look.

RAY. What look is that?

MOLLY. Tortured. Slightly ripped; beneath your shirt.

RAY. You like the slightly-ripped/tortured look?

MOLLY. Yeah, it's kinda my thing.

RAY. As opposed to slightly tortured/*totally* ripped?

MOLLY. Yeah, if it's too ripped it detracts from the torture. Don't wanna tip the scales.

RAY. Gotcha. (*Pause.*) You know, that day, when we were up in
    the lifeguard stand and we were kissing, I remember you had
    some pizza sauce stuck in the corner of your mouth.

MOLLY. I did?

RAY. Yeah, and I didn't wanna tell you because I thought it
    might embarrass you.

MOLLY. Jesus, that's horrible.

RAY. No, it was nice. Plus I ended up sort of licking it off, so –

MOLLY. Yeeeww –

RAY. No, it was tasty, that place had the best sauce in town.

MOLLY. Is the place not still there – ?

RAY. No actually, it is, yeah –

MOLLY. Do you still go?

RAY. No, I don't.

MOLLY. Why not?

RAY. I just, you know, I gotta stay slightly ripped –

MOLLY. We should go for breakfast!

RAY. No –

MOLLY. Yes! – is it open?

RAY. I doubt it –

MOLLY. Let's go try, c'mon, Ray, for ole times' sake –

RAY. I really don't wanna go –

MOLLY. Why not?

RAY. Because –

MOLLY. Why?

RAY. I dunno –

MOLLY. Did you once see a rat in the kitchen – ?

RAY. No –

MOLLY. A dead seagull?

RAY. No –

MOLLY. So why? –

RAY. I just have bad memories of it; *not* the time with you, but in general.

Beat as MOLLY *suddenly realises what he's referring to.*

MOLLY. Oh.

Beat.

Is that… is it where you went to eat pizza for twenty-five minutes after what happened?

RAY. Yeah.

MOLLY *takes this in for a moment.*

MOLLY. Well, *that's* fun.

RAY. Can we not talk about it?

MOLLY. Okay.

Beat.

RAY. Listen to me: the night it happened, I did not feel. You're wondering what was going through my mind for those twenty-five minutes? – the answer is nothing. I was not *feeling*. At all. Even as I knew he was lying there bleeding from his head, I made myself not see it and not feel it. And the entire point of my life, if there is a point, since then, has been *to* feel. Because I know that by *lacking* it that night, I destroyed. So I try to feel. Which is maybe even why – if you wanna get – which is why I asked you out to coffee, and to dinner, is because you are someone that I can, who I can – this is dumb – who I can *feel* about. I felt it the day we kissed when we were kids, I felt it when I kissed you the other day, I felt it last night, I'm feeling it now. This is fucking corny but I'm saying it so here it is. Okay? So please; *please* don't

think of me always in that – or do, but don't let it stop you
from, even just *considering* me as someone who is
potentially someone who could... who you could, *whom* you
could eventually – *see* again. *Please*... don't let it do that.

MOLLY....I won't.

(*To audience*.) But I do.

RAY (*to audience*). She does. She never calls again.

    MOLLY *with* RAY*; later.*

MOLLY. I'll call you.

RAY. Okay.

MOLLY. Thank you for breakfast.

RAY. It was my pleasure.

MOLLY. And for last night.

RAY. Of course –

MOLLY. Not just the dinner, but the, the whole night.

RAY. Me too. I mean, *I* thank *you*.

MOLLY. Do you have stuff to do today?

RAY. Ah, yeah, I'm supposed to meet a guy who's gonna help
me do a website for my company, so... What about you?

MOLLY. I actually have to head into the office.

RAY. On a Sunday?

MOLLY. Yeah, my boss, Jeff, is, he's very – he *loves* having me
work on Sundays.

    They regard each other...

So... Will we – you have my number, right?

RAY. Yeah –

MOLLY. So maybe we'll talk, whenever?

RAY. I'd like that.

MOLLY. Me too.

RAY. Okay.

MOLLY. Okay, Ray.

RAY. Okay.

Beat.

MOLLY *turns away… and speaks to audience, slow at first.*

MOLLY. The thing with me is… that I'm in communications. And I need the people in my life… to have that too. (*Pause.*) Not that Ray doesn't. He's actually pretty good, in terms of what he is now – and who he wasn't then; and I think he even means it. (*Pause.*) But what he *can't* do… is make me understand. Because what he *did* – at its core – remains a complete fucking mystery to me. And so while I have sympathy… (*Strong.*) I *do not* have empathy. (*Looking for the thought.*) Which I know is ironic, seeing as only two years before that… that same kid somehow made me recognise the version of myself that I wanted the world to see. It was *Ray* – hat on backwards and eyes inside my heart – for whom I stripped myself of armour and kissed as the sun went down. (*Emphatic.*) Which is *why* I can stand here and say, 'If there was *ever* a chance for me, if I *ever* had it made, it was right then and there on that lifeguard chair – with Ray from Rehoboth Beach.' (*Pause.*) And *that* is fucking true.

Beat. RAY *speaks to audience.*

RAY. That letter she wrote to herself? I'd actually found it a long time ago. It was the year after she and I kissed, and I had a part-time job helping the caretaker on that house, and he'd asked me to check the insulation and I'd found this note and remembered the name Molly from the summer before. (*Pause.*) And when I read it, at the end she asked herself if she was happy, in the future. And I turned it over and wrote 'No.' (*Pause.*) Which I did because… I think because I was mad that she'd never written *me* a letter. Because I remembered that afternoon we'd spent together and I think I was just pissed she'd never written. I think I thought she must be a summer snob; didn't wanna have anything to do with the locals except for during vacation. (*Pause*.) Anyway, when it came up again, I didn't remember at first, and when I did, I didn't mention it. Because I was too embarrassed to tell her I'd written such a stupid response.

I never see her again. Which is not – out of the blue. I had thought... that maybe she had 'heard' me. Or seen; or whatever they say. I had tried to express myself, which I wasn't in the habit of, because it's usually not worth it.

And I guess it wasn't; I guess she couldn't get past the cowardice. (*Beat*.) Anyway. Life ploughs on. The rest of our lives will look normal. Probably. Molly will die of brain cancer at age fifty-nine, which will be way too early and sad.

I'll live to the dumb and undeserved age of ninety-two, the difference in our life spans being a simple nod to absurdity. My last dying breaths will be difficult for me to catch, and there in my demented mind will be those kids yelling at me to 'Die you withered old faggot, die.' (*Pause*.) And *maybe* my last thought, in fifty-two years, will be of Molly, and her lips that taste like syrup, even though I'll know full well that the key to life isn't a kiss or a sunset or a lifeguard stand at dusk; but as I tremble, the death march on its way, that little unattached image might float through my unconscious, maybe even sneaking into my thoughts, the focus of my brain for maybe half a second, even as those kids are yelling 'Faggot'. And it might rest there on my eyelids: she and I on that lifeguard stand. (*Pause*.) Or not.

The lights shift to dusk; perhaps an utterly real lifeguard stand appears on stage. MOLLY and RAY slowly climb it, kissing with the zealousness that young teenagers tend to kiss with; they are age fifteen and sixteen though they don't necessarily act 'young'. After several moments, MOLLY breaks the kiss off suddenly.

MOLLY. It's nice up here.

RAY. It's gorgeous.

MOLLY. Did you just say 'gorgeous'?

RAY. Why, does this sound dumb?

MOLLY. A *little* bit.

RAY. Sorry –

MOLLY. No, it's nice; it's cool.

RAY. Yeah?

MOLLY. Totally.

RAY. Cool.

MOLLY. It's true; it's gorgeous right now; especially from up here.

    Beat.

RAY. Every now and then, I have, like, one of these moments, when I'm in a place like this, usually when I'm alone or with very few people around, when everything just sort of, like, slows down, and it's all really… gorgeous, and it's like I understand things.

MOLLY. What things?

RAY. I dunno. But more than that just with my mom, or school. I'm talking about things like… that the entire balance of the universe… is gonna be okay.

MOLLY. Really?

RAY. Yeah.

    Looking at him seriously; genuine.

MOLLY. That's really cool.

RAY. Thanks.

    MOLLY *leans over and kisses him for a couple long seconds. Beat.*

    You're pretty…

MOLLY. Confident?

RAY. Yeah.

MOLLY. I know. (*Pause*.) I'm an all-powerful, all-knowing, all-loving woman.

RAY. Nice.

MOLLY. I plan to rule the universe.

RAY. Sweet.

MOLLY. I plan to have thirteen children but not be slowed down by them. And I'm going to be a supreme and healthy nutritionist. And possibly the first female US senator to be both into nutrition *and* child-raising *and* publishing books of fucking totally gorgeous poetry.

RAY (*regards her, impressed*). That's pretty sweet.

MOLLY. I know.

RAY. Thirteen kids, huh?

MOLLY. Yep.

RAY. You might run out of good names.

MOLLY. Not a worry, they're all gonna be named Roof. Short for Rufus.

RAY. Even the girls?

MOLLY. *Especially*.

RAY. Have you always been like this?

MOLLY. Yes. (*Beat*.) For the last year.

RAY. What were you like before last year?

MOLLY. Well, for one thing, I stuttered.

RAY. *Really?*

MOLLY. Yeah.

RAY. You don't seem like you would stutter.

MOLLY. That's because I'm a supreme and all-powerful woman.

RAY.…I don't think I've ever met someone who stuttered.

MOLLY. You probably have, but maybe not the one who *still* stuttered.

RAY. True. (*Beat*.) That's cool. That you stopped.

MOLLY. Thanks.

Beat. RAY *kisses her on the lips one time, gently.*

RAY. You must have like a thousand guys who wanna date you.

MOLLY. No.

RAY. Yeah, you do, you're one of those girls, I can tell –

MOLLY. I'm not –

RAY. Yeah, you are –

MOLLY. Guys don't like me.

RAY. Why?

MOLLY. 'Cause I'm too extreme –

RAY. Oh right –

MOLLY. I'm serious.

RAY. I believe you –

MOLLY. Good, because it's t– it's… true.

Beat.

RAY. Was that for real?

No answer.

Did you just stutter?

MOLLY. Fuck.

RAY. You weren't joking?

MOLLY. Goddam it –

RAY. It's totally not a big deal.

MOLLY. But I haven't *done* it in a year.

RAY. It doesn't matter, it's just one time, it was like half a second.

MOLLY. *Shit.*

RAY. Molly?

MOLLY. What?

RAY. It doesn't matter. It doesn't. I swear. It was probably just a freak occurrence.

No answer.

Molly?

MOLLY. Maybe.

RAY. Hey.

He very gently takes her head in his hands, so that she is looking at him; then he very slowly kisses her forehead.

Molly; you've got it made. I swear.

MOLLY *looks at him and smiles.*

MOLLY (*near whisper*). Thank you, Ray.

RAY.... You got it.

They sit together... as lights slowly fade.

The End.

A Nick Hern Book

Dusk Rings A Bell first published in Great Britain in 2011 as a paperback original by Nick Hern Books Limited, 14 Larden Road, London W3 7ST, in association with HighTide Festival Theatre

Cover image by Nick Warren | www.n9design.com
Cover design by Ned Hoste, 2H

Typeset by Nick Hern Books, London
Printed in Great Britain by CLE Print Ltd, St Ives, Cambs, PE27 3LE

ISBN 978 1 84842 201 8

A CIP catalogue record for this book is available from the British Library